Nameless as the Minnows

Poems

Praise for *Nameless as the Minnows*:

In *Nameless as the Minnows*, Connie Jordan Green calls forth all the power and strength of the elegiac form to examine the most foundational mysteries of what it means to be "migrants formed from stardust but not yet of the heavens." This paradox that defines the human condition is illuminated by Green's lifetime of personal experiences, from her memories of girlhood, through her early years of marriage and parenthood, and finally to the awareness that her own "memory and breath" are destined to dim. All of Green's work shines with the same light she describes in a portrait of a young girl peeling potatoes—the kind of light that might be the sun rising but may just as easily be the sun setting. Regardless, we are all the better for basking in the glow.

—Denton Loving, author of *Tamp*

Lush and wholehearted, Connie Green's masterful new book of poems, *Nameless as the Minnows*, is a must-have collection of northern accents, southern drawls, cars, boats, birds, stars, cups of tea, potato peels, and prayer. "Bless the dirty / knees, the tangled hair of my everyday self," she writes in a language "slow [as a] river / you would paddle all day," building a symphony of memories orchestrating a time and location where "they fry chicken for our dinner, / pile us kids all into one bed, the cows returning at day's end." Green's throaty verse illuminates the grit and unflinching spirit of rural America, each carefully crafted line skillfully depicting the power of family and the pride and comfort that can be drawn from the people and places we call home.

—Kari Gunter-Seymour, Ohio Poet Laureate,
author of *Dirt Songs*

In *Nameless as the Minnows*, internal momentum drives Connie Jordan Green's new collection backward and forward as the speaker expresses "the rhythm of our lives." Though the speaker is keenly mindful that she and her kin are "nearing the end of the knowable," her memories are not vignetted in sentimentalized mist but vividly reproduced. As the title of one poem attests, Green is devoted to "Ars Specifica"—the art of paying attention to quotidian details. Though at times the tone may be elegiac, we don't meet ghosts but lived experiences. Readers meet not girlhood but the girl in body and spirit, not the wife's vague nostalgia but "the enormity of love." Every scintilla is of awakening as the speaker's memories continue to transform her gratitude. This book testifies that aging is not anathema to fascination and childlike wonder. Green is masterful as she puts us into the skin which covers not her static self-portrait, but the still-shifting pulse of dynamic living.

—Susan O'Dell Underwood, author of *Splinter*
and *Genesis Road*

"[I]f we were allowed to choose / our miracles," Connie Jordan Green proposes in her latest collection, *Nameless as the Minnows*, even as she testifies of miracles found everywhere she looks—in family, in garden, in memory, even in language itself. Out of mystery and back into mystery, she embraces and accepts the known, the unknown, and even the unknowable. Spine-stiffened, prayerfully attentive, born of mountain ancestors, hers is a voice of a soul at peace, sharpened by a mind conditioned, out of necessity, to look at absence, loss, deprivation, or need and then to get busy doing the hard work of wrestling blessing from—and offering blessing for—this unkempt, unquenchable, sometimes dwindling, often unbearable, always sacred space we share.

—Jeff Hardin, author of *Watermark* and *A Clearing Space
in the Middle of Being*

Also by Connie Jordan Green:

Poems

Darwin's Breath (Iris Publishing Group, Inc., 2018)

Household Inventory (Brick Road Press,
    Brick Road Poetry Prize, 2015)

Regret Comes to Tea (Finishing Line Press, 2011)

Slow Children Playing (Finishing Line Press, 2007)

Novels

Emmy (Macmillan Publishing Company, 1992;
    reissued by Iris Publishing Group, Inc., 2008)

The War at Home (Macmillan Publishing Company,
    1989; reissued by Iris Publishing Group, Inc., 2003)

Nameless as the Minnows

Poems

Connie Jordan Green

MAD**V**ILLE
PUBLISHING

LAKE DALLAS, TEXAS

Requests for permission to reprint or reuse material
from this work should be sent to:

Permissions
Madville Publishing
PO Box 358
Lake Dallas, TX 75065

Cover Photo and Design: Jacqueline Davis
Author Photo: Megan Morris Photography

ISBN: 978-1-963695-29-8 paperback
978-1-963695-30-4 ebook
Library of Congress Control Number: 2024941527

These poems are dedicated to family and friends, teachers and students—those gone from this good green Earth and those still present—who have traveled with me along life's joyous journey.

Contents

I.

II.

III.

I.

Poetry gives the griever not release from
grief but companionship in grief.

—Donald Hall

Nameless as the Minnows

Into lake waters I ease my pale body.
I am nine years old, conscious of the way
water climbs my legs, embraces my stomach,

though I don't yet realize this touch is like
that of a lover I will someday know, someone
yet nameless, faceless, formless. For now

I have only sun to caress my shoulders, only
the thrum of a distant fisherman's outboard motor
to sing my blood into its familiar rhythm, breath

caught by the chill water, and I am yet nameless
as the silvery scaled minnows glinting through
the shallows, always just beyond my reach,

ripples washing me through another day
toward that faceless future, my reflection
in the water a brighter self I have yet to meet.

What Never Happened

The witch your aunt said lived in the front room
never grabbed you with her long green fingernails,
her hands like the claws on Grandmother's chickens.

The mine whistle never blew long and loud,
a knife through the summer afternoon,
and the neighbor didn't shoot the dog

everyone declared was rabid, the dog
writhing in the dusty road, a cloud
of flies already formed overhead.

If dreams washed you through the dark hours,
they were never as real as your terror of the wall
of water roaring down the creek bed after spring rains.

Summers were never as long as you thought,
mosquitoes and ticks that scavenged on your
arms and legs less than a barbarian horde,

and you always awakened to sheets smelling
of sunshine, the sound of your father opening
a kitchen cupboard, everyone you loved sheltered

beneath the roof over your bed, though the stars
were shut out and language was a slow river
you would paddle all day.

First Death

We were gathered around the coal grate,
eyes focused on our grandmother
like compass needles on due north.
She was cutting paperdolls from newspaper,
a string of human figures linked together,
hand-to-hand, elegant as ballerinas,
as connected as my cousins, my sisters and I,
cross-legged on the linoleum floor.
December rain beat at the windows,
wind swirled drafts of smoke down
into the room, Christmas carols flowed
from the Philco in the corner—and then
my mother, my aunts and uncles opened
the door and walked in. Cold, that obscene
intruder, entered with them, the words *he's gone*
like ice pellets driven on the storm of their arrival.
The universe opened a black hole, swallowed
our small room as Grandmother's scissors
clattered to the floor and she slid from the chair
into the arms of her grandchildren.

Moving to Tennessee, 1944

after Mary Morris

Goodbye to cousins, grandparents, coal tipple
and craggy mountains, smoke from smoldering
slag heaps. We have packed the car with pillows,
blankets, tucked the dog into his box,
called the movers for the couch and chairs.

Hello to towering peaks of ancient Cherokee
lands, to clear rivers and calm lakes, the puzzle
of a fenced city. Hello to strangers living
in the other end of our house, to hearing
unknown voices through the walls.

We are a city of nomads, Maine to
New Mexico, Oregon to Florida, former
coal miners and white-coated scientists.
We wander muddy roads, stand in lines
for coffee, sugar, save gasoline rationing
coupons for fuel to travel back home
where they fry chicken for our dinner,
pile us kids all into one bed, spread sheets
over the living room daybed for the adults.

We have traveled too far to truly return,
migrants formed from stardust but not
yet of the heavens. Someday we will
journey through constellations, gaze
upon the Earth, a misty blue sphere
floating in a dark sea. And we will
weep for the fragility of such a home.

Car Trip

Somewhere in the rain
and mist of a winter day
you travel with your family—
those souls who have fled
still united in the gray Ford,
your father's cigarette smoke
eddying around your head,
your stomach turning, nausea
as dizzying as the steep mountains,
your mother's cool hand
passing you a lemon slice,
the bitter bite of it like a fresh
wind that pushes down the bile,
and once more the world
is icicles hanging from stone
outcroppings, battered houses
clinging to the mountainsides,
the car turning, turning,
curves and drop-offs lurching
past like dreams that sometimes
pursue you through the night—
but for those few hours all
you hold dear secure in that car
making its way from shadow
into sunlight.

The Worker's Story

One a.m. and I've just come off the evening shift,
everyone I know asleep in bed except my working
companions. Steam rises behind us as we board
the bus back to town, the plant a giant that seems
still only from the outside—cauldrons and motors
rumbling and roaring, the eternal processes running
around the clock, other men and women
there now to keep the beast breathing.

I'm off to bed, will crawl in beside my wife, the feel
of her hip against mine what is left of those years
when desire drove us like pistons, our young daughters
asleep in the next room, the house a universe unto itself,
rising and falling through the long night while
the Milky Way lays its road across the heavens.

Those Others

On the radio *Amos n' Andy*,
the thick dialect bringing
peals of laughter from my parents,
years before we three girls
would know the words *racism*,
prejudice, our lives a pattern

of rising in the morning
to a neighborhood of children
who looked like us, sitting
in classrooms with white children,
teachers, a one-dimensional life
we never questioned, our own

differences we thought a rich
mixture of northern accents,
southern drawls, children from
the coalfields beside those from
New York City, children of doctors,
physicists, teachers, fathers and mothers

who turned the dials on machines
whose purpose no one knew until
the bomb dropped on those others,
the ones with the slanted eyes,
our world still a cocoon, our sleep
deep as the hills walling in our town.

Bless It All

Bless the pastel dresses, the new hats
of my childhood Easters, meant to turn me
into a lady in one day. Bless the dirty
knees, the tangled hair of my everyday self.
Bless the new doll on Christmas morning,
the boys in Sunday School class I watched
while my head was bowed. Bless the folded hands
of ladies in church, their nail polish bright.

Bless all the things that held me in the holy—
the hunger that lasted through the sermon,
the hard pews. Bless the wooden church on
the hill where my grandmother took my sisters
and me, the fear of fire the preacher shouted.
Bless my grandmother who shook with laughter.

The Family That Dances Together

Mother's quickstep to the music, the way
her body was shaped of grace notes and jazziness—

my father's clumsy attempts to lead her, though his feet knew
only the plod of plow and tramp of cows returning at day's end—

my sisters and I twirling our makeshift tutus of towels
tied at our waists, as we leap again and again, imaginary

ballets our minds construct from the nothingness of radio
static shrouding the music that stuttered through our living room—

though this morning birds chorus their own melodies,
set my spirit to dance again with those long-ago figures.

Tell Me About Driving

Tell me about the first time you slid
behind the wheel of a car, how the seat
scratched the back of your legs, or was it
summer, the seat black vinyl, your legs
sticking to the vinyl? And then your dad
said *push in the clutch and turn the key*
and you did and the engine fired on all
cylinders and you felt the rumble of power
under your hands and you thought how
you had lived all your life waiting
for this moment—and then he said
ease off the clutch while you give it a little gas,
and the car bucked and the engine coughed
and died, and nothing was easy anymore
as you tried again and flooded the engine,
and you thought maybe you would just walk
the remainder of your life, and then one day
you were driving, rolling along the highway,
one arm propped in the window, pine trees
dropping their soft needles on you, the sun
a beacon pulling you down the long road.

Learning to Shift Gears

Beside him on the front seat of the gray
Frazier Manhattan, I learned about gears,
the trick of easing off the clutch without
killing the motor, though for weeks my attempts
created a bucking bronco my dad and I rode
the way my sisters and I rode our stick ponies
around our bumpy backyard, legs chafing
against the bamboo poles my dad had cut
on the riverbank, cut for his beans, supports
for vines that would bloom with bud and nub
and long slender pods our mother would blanch
and cram into jars, pressure cooker steaming
the kitchen, quarts of beans our winter fodder,
my sisters and me outgrowing stick ponies,
learning stick shifts, our dad beside us as the road
smoothed to gray asphalt we rolled over at twenty,
thirty, forty miles an hour, the future a destination
we never envisioned, sitting beside him
on the front seat of the old Frazier Manhattan.

Witness

They smoke beneath a side canopy
or sheltered by the passageway
between classrooms and gym.
They are not bad, only wild
with the fierceness of youth,
reckless on hormones and longing.
In later years they will marry,
own their own garage or teach
math to boys as rebellious
as they once were. For now
they cup their hands to tent
the match against the wind, inhale
morning's first taste of nicotine,
exhale a cloud that settles on clothing
and in hair, scent that clings
through English, history classes,
where girls in starched white blouses
move to the far side of the room,
secretly eye the rebels
while they feign attention to the text
before them, bid the dreams
sleep will bring, their own
wildness a banked fire, embers
glowing in the dark, waiting
for love's warm breath.

Clothes Drying in the Sun

My sister and I stand by the washer
feeding sheets through the wringer rollers, fat
lengths of fabric flattened into pastel
boards we'll pin to the clothesline where wind
and sun will restore the softness we'll spread
on our bed, our parents' bed, our younger
sister's bed, sleep that will knit the raveled
edge of day, the bard wrote, his own lines hung
with color we still mine some four hundred
years later, my sister and I gone on
to lives striped and streaked and mottled, rainbow
hues wavering before eyes that someday
will dim along with memory and breath and
the sweet joy of clothes drying in the sun.

Portrait of a Young Girl Peeling Potatoes

In her right hand the knife, wingtip
extension of her bone structure.
Her thin fingers wrap the handle,
thumb guides the blade, peel separates
from potato flesh. Spots on the back
of her hand are dark as the shadow
her bent head casts over the bowl
of water, cradle for each skinless potato.

Somewhere off to her right
light is breaking, the sun ascending.
Or could it be evening, the last
rays to illumine her labor?

McCrory's Five and Ten

It is always midday in McCrory's Five and Ten,
the overhead florescent bulbs bright as the sun,
though only the front windows let us know
what weather approaches. I am sixteen,
my first real job, standing behind the toy counter
taking dimes and nickels in exchange for small cars,
wooden paddles with balls attached by rubber strings,
coloring books, boxes of Crayolas.

Across the room the popcorn popper pops
its ratchety ditty, smell of butter and corn
mingle with the aroma of oiled hardwood floors,
while the same Johnny Cash record sings
all day to those of us gathered within the store's
walls, Cash continually walking the line because,
he insists, you—collectively, individually—are mine.

But I am in charge of the young, my pocket filled
with pennies for the cash register, for who
under the age of ten knows about sales tax?

Beyond the lights, the ceiling peaks in dark shadows
as we move through our day—bag, make change,
punch our time cards as we come and go, walk
home in the gathering dusk, the future somewhere
beyond, the children's eager eyes, their hands reaching.

Tell Me How You Were Wild and Green in the Ways of the World

And I will tell you about my wildness, my greenness—
how every morning dawned like a new creation,
how fountains spurted in the sunlight,
rainbows arched and vanished like the days,
how we never knew years could go like scenes
flashing past a train window,
how we stood before the schoolhouse door
when summer ended with its salt and sweat and prickles,
how we would walk the long hallways, books clutched
to our chests, voices and laughter surrounding us,
each of us a cocoon where time spun her spell—
girl into woman mysterious as a butterfly chrysalis—
how we couldn't know the secret of being still
and waiting, and time rolled us down the years.

Title of poem borrowed from a prompt in Natalie Goldberg's *Old Friend from Far Away*, 2007

Looking Back

the shrill whistle
of my father's cupped hands

calling my sisters and me from play,
summoning us from the vacant lot
behind the government's Cemesto

houses, hear it in the summer rain
on our porch roof where we swapped
comics with neighborhood children,

hear it in my mother's song, steam
frizzing her hair while she ironed
ruffle, pleat, and tucks of our cotton

dresses, know my youth in the scent
of corn tasseling in a backyard garden,
dust of chalkboard, sweat of gym clothes,

pungent chlorine of summer swims,
touch the years of youth in sun-dried
sheets and paste-waxed floors, a life

that flowed with the years,
seamless as a stream wearing
away rock, carving its bed.

There Was: An Elegy for My Father

There was the black dirt he created by carting
loads of manure from a farm near our fenced city.
There was the hoe, handle roughened by weather
and use, his grip on it as sure as his hold on all tools,
as his wielding of the knife that sliced chicken leg
free from back and breast. There was the way he
and hoe opened furrows in the dark earth, his rough
hand dropping seeds into my open palm, his trust
I would place each seed three inches from its neighbor.

When he lay beneath the pink-shaded lights,
the smell of chrysanthemums sickening the air,
the ruffled satin around his head and torso
more foreign than anything life had offered,
there were his hands folded on his chest.

The Question of Where

It was the winter after your death,
darkness coming early, a shadow
that lingered until late morning,
my days spent gazing out the window,
my mind never leaving the question
of where. You had been so present,
how could you be gone, and to where—
to out beyond the hills, over the lakes
of our summers, beneath the soil
of your gardening days? Where, where,
my brain tugged the question from
morning till evening. My hands found
work in the mixing, stirring, pushing,
pulling of breadmaking, a new pursuit
that filled the long hours, the rhythm
of rising and resting and rising again
a song that sang me through winter days
until light waxed us into spring, earth
greened and the where of my searching
quieted into the steady beat of my heart.

Earth, Always Earth

after Cecilia Woloch

If the garden were a sky filled with stars,
if the sky shone with sunlight and then
the luster of five hundred billion stars
swimming in our Milky Way, and if you
were the garden, if you each spring could
return, resurrected from the dark earth,
grown anew from the richness of compost
and fungi and all that eats and morphs
and dies and becomes and returns and enriches—
if the garden were more than metaphor
for hope, if the garden—where you spent
your hours, where your back glistened
with the sweat of labor, with the saving
salt of life—if we were allowed to choose
our miracles—I would walk out on an April
morning and find you, oh my father, find
you where your soul was most at peace,
find you in the early light—my father
returned as the earth returns to itself,
year after year after blessed year.

Elegy for My Mother

I drive away from the nursing home, round
the bend where daylilies flash yellow and
orange, car windows open. June air lifts my hair,
erases scent of nursing home, image
of walkers and wheelchairs, beds cranked
so the bedridden can watch the world.

Children call from a swing set, dogs race
in full voice along a chain-link fence.
I tune the radio to the oldies station,
song springs from the static—*my buddy,*
your buddy misses you, and I pull to the curb,
put my head on the steering wheel, weep
for your life—you two years yet away from dying.

On Not Remembering

in memory of my sister Sue (1940-2018)

Who needs this March day, wind a winter howl,
this gray day when daffodils regret their
early unfolding. Who needs smoke from chimneys,
children wrapped in scarves and hats, a woman

wiping fog from her car window, the engine
growling beneath the hood. Who needs the ambulance
in the night, a hospital room with its
glaring light, the ropes of tubes that tethered you.

I had in mind a June day, you in shorts,
sandals, cutting red roses from the rambler
by the door. Or a quiet evening, sunset
painting the lake pink and orange, water lapping
our toes, a canoe creaking against the dock,
all we ever needed gathered in one small spot.

Eight Ways of Looking at Loss

I.
What we've lost lingers
like fog over the river.

II.
What we've lost cradles us
like our mother's arms.

III.
What we've lost retreats
like a face in a rearview mirror.

IV.
What we've lost swoops
like a nighthawk scooping insects.

V.
What we've lost echoes in the cry
of children playing at twilight.

VI.
What we've lost dances before us
like young girls at their first ballet.

VII.
What we've lost hides in the shadows
of the last dream before morning.

VIII.
What we've lost is neither lost nor absent
but is exhaled with each breath, settles
in our bones the way sand calcifies into stone.

II.

All poems are elegies at their core.

—Maxine Kumin

Hungry for Love

I was too young to know
  the cause of my hunger.

I ate all day—a snack
  before breakfast, again

midmorning, midafternoon,
  just before bed, three solid

meals filling in the time gaps.
  I was ribs and sharp hip bones,

gangly arms and narrow wrists.
  My body shed fat like a dog

shaking off water. Even my dreams
  were a banquet snatched away

before I took the first bite.
  Not until I found you

did flesh find its nourishment—
  a feast of marbled muscle,

juicy earlobes, lips of honey,
  sweet neck for nibbling,

my own body filling out,
  curves where angles had defined

my space, a jagged landscape
  dissolved into smooth hills

and long green meadows,
  rich with all I needed for survival.

Moving to the Country

It was our first winter on the farm,
twenty-five-year-olds with a one-year-
old, another on the way. The farmhouse
was small, uninsulated, a cold water
spigot in the kitchen, light bulb dangling
from the ceiling in each of the four rooms,
no heating system. We added a bath
in the corner of the kitchen, stapled

plastic to the windows, piled firewood
on the porch and hunkered down.
Mid-October, cold set in, temperatures
started a slow slide that would last
into late March. In early December, water
froze in the toilet bowl, snow swirled
around the house. All winter

wind moaned in the chimney, bent
the cedars like hapless wanderers bowing
in supplication before a god who paid
no mind to anyone's troubles. When
the first daffodil popped through spring's
thawing soil, we emerged into a world
we had forgotten existed—warm sun
on our faces like the kiss of a long-lost lover.

Watching

In those days there was no time or money
for filling feeders to lure the bright birds
close to the house, but still they came—
scarlet cardinals, sky-tinted bluebirds,
raucous jays, companionable brown wrens
and sparrows of various stripes and specklings.

That first year we wrapped the old house
in plastic—faint effort to seal out the cold—
watched the wintry world waver and swim,
the presence of birds a surprise each time
we stepped outdoors. They came for maple
seeds, berries on the dogwoods, blue fruit
of cedars, they fending for themselves,
depending upon DNA shaped through eons,

our small family huddled nearby, only
the sturdy stock of our mountain ancestors
stiffening our spines for each day's wood
chopping, fire building, the coming chore
of breaking earth and planting seed for what
would sustain us year by year by year.

Dish Towel

after Ann Quinn

Wave in the summer breeze
like a field of ripe wheat,
light as a baby's hair,
flatter than a pancake.

Lie quietly in the drawer
with your kin,
kiss the moisture
from the dinner plates.

Child of the flour sack,
cousin to the bathroom hand towel,
grandmother to rags
in the cleaning closet.

O cotton boiled and beaten,
bleached by sun,
pounded and struck
on river rocks.

O memory holder
of childhood chores,
song of my daily trek—
stove to table to sink.

You who neither ask
nor answer, you
who just are
and shall be.

My Sister Points Out the Obvious

You chose to live this way,
she reminds me when
the water pump freezes,
windows rattle in the wind,
cold seeps through the walls like
water pouring through a sieve,
the power is off for days
after a summer storm,
neighbors helping each
other out when trees fall
onto the road, a tractor slips
into the pond, cows die
while giving birth. We chose
to live miles from the nearest
house, a long drive to doctor
or store, church or movie. We
choose in summer to sit
on the deck, birds for music,
distant mountains for view,
choose winter solace of warm
hearth, a bed piled high
with quilts, the soft sound
of our breathing filling the night.

Rocks

[O]ur rocks / flourished with no attention at all.
—Jesse Graves

Our first and most lasting harvest was rocks—
rocks we picked up across the pasture fields,
heaved onto an open wagon hitched to the small
Farmall that chugged up the hills we had bought
as farm, rocks we unloaded to fill gullies
that rivered our ground, remnants of poor farming
practices and still poorer soil, a purchase we
in ignorance eagerly made, the yearning for
our own land a light that brightened those days
of clay-locked earth flailed with hoe, bean and tomato
plants doomed to struggle while we stubbornly
hauled rock after rock to a place in the shade
where only the lizards, occasional snake
saw their beauty and rejoiced in the abundant crop.

Help

Along a wall in my husband's workshop
hang the saws—handsaws, bow saws,
a crosscut saw stretched above the display,
jigsaws beneath a work bench, hole saws.

A radial-arm saw hulks in the corner.
There are hammers of all sizes, hefts,
and ages, plus countless screwdrivers,
channel locks, pliers, levels, carpenter

squares, nails, screws, brads, measuring
instruments—yardsticks, tapes, calipers,
scales—help for any chores that plague
our days. And yet, when the door sags

on its hinges, we stuff old socks
in the resultant crack. When a floorboard
loosens, we pull the rug over the offending
plank. When a faucet develops a leak,

we learn to sleep to the music of the drip.
In the workshop, the tools hang
through summer heat and the cold
of winter. Sunlight peeks in grimy

windows, rain gurgles in the downspouts.
The tools live their solitary lives
neither humbled nor exalted,
help a few steps away.

Feeding

I wake to the sound of a tractor
chugging across the field.
Feeding time. And I remember
those first years, how the cows
called us each evening, silhouetted
against a metal sky, vapor rising
with each bellow. How you
shed suit and white shirt, pulled on
boots and jeans, headed for the barn,
our young son in tow. How each
evening you split firewood, stacked
it on the porch, how all day I lugged
logs to our small fireplace, the house
a cave we tried to heat, those children
we fed, warmed, gave what love
we knew to give, how the days lingered
into dusk and dark, and we fell asleep
to the sound of wind at the corners,
woke once more to hungry cattle,
hungry children, the rhythm of our lives.

Tractor

Let those gears that shifted
for hill and row and blade
and rake and baler,

the tires that rolled over
timothy and lespedeza
and thistle and daisies,

that steering wheel where
generations of hands twisted
and clung and rested,

the exhaust pipe
that belched dark smoke,
the chassis that held all together—

let all that worked and labored
in sun and rain, in heat
and winter storm now rest

in the shelter of the leaning barn,
now slowly return to rust and oxygen
beneath the wide arms of the barnyard oak.

To Sleeplessness

I am prisoner of the stopped
   clock hands, thrall
      to the crack of light

beneath the bedroom door,
   chained by the gentle snore
      of my sound-asleep husband.

I am captive to the owl's hoot
   somewhere beyond the barn,
      the skitter of mice in the kitchen cupboard,

the list of haven't-dones that waves
   like a flag, warning sleep
      away from my bed,

bound tight by thoughts
   that might as well be
      toothpicks propping my eyelids.

Chicken Psalm

after Lisa Bellamy

To the earnest eaters of shelled
corn, chickweed tossed into their pen,

to the pickers among the kitchen
scraps—melon rinds, wilted lettuce leaves,

to contented hens snug on their
nests and the smooth eggs they warm,

to frenzied hens herding their chicks
through barnyards, I say, *Blessings,*

for they keep their mind on business,
have no time for frolicking, for dozing

behind the hay bales; they care
nothing for gentle entreaties, come only

to grain flung like the stars of a distant
galaxy by a woman in work boots and

a sun bonnet. Forgetting the weasel,
the fox too clever for fences and closed

doors, they work at living—grain
and other good things in, eggs out—

these givers who live without
contemplation, philosophy,

who have no need for one more ode
to their feathery perfection.

Trust as Synonym for Gardener

What else to call it when you drop
seeds into furrows where only a few
days earlier crystals of frost shone
in the early sunlight? What other
label to apply to those who would
bet everything on the coming of rain,
the steadiness of sun, who are willing
to risk beetle and deer, aphids
and raccoons, who put their faith
in the reliability of the seasons,
the strength of their own backs,
who year after year return
to the work they love.

Scattered

I have become a lazy gardener,
happy for nature to do much of my work.
In October I intend to deadhead
zinnias and marigolds, cut back
stems of hibiscus, pull up cleome
and Mexican sunflower, tidy my garden
the way I did years ago when a day
of bending was no more challenging
than a day of vacuuming or baking.
In midwinter I urge myself to prune
the grapevines and apple trees.

Daily, while I promise labor tomorrow,
birds visit my dormant garden, feast
on seed and berry, shake the stalks
and brush against winged seeds,
a scattering that guarantees summer's
zinnia and marigold, cleome and sunflower.
While I plan to get busy soon, grapevines
crawl into the arms of the redbud
where they will feed birds and squirrels,
all my gardeners who wish to eat
summer, winter, spring, or fall.

Change Coming

One would think the year's activity
dwindling now that October slips away
and the last tomato vines hang dry
and dying in the ruined garden. But
there along the fence, autumn clematis
opens its white blooms, a smell so sweet
the bees forget their fall tasks and frolic
among the flowers as if on the first day
of spring. And look how the groundhog
fattens on persimmons dropping like rain
from a tree that is all limbs and orange
fruit against the blue sky. Neighbors
mow neglected fields, machines
pushing through briers and thistles,
a housecleaning of sorts meant to set
the farm to rights before those of us
in the country close our doors, light
the logs laid on the hearth last April.
Soon enough we will all sleep.

The December Bee

flies around my kitchen
flirts with the heat of the range,
finds neither shrub nor flowering vine:

I knead the bread,
stir the soup,
avoid the brush of his wings,

until my daughter grabs
a cup, napkin,
scoops and seals him,

opens the kitchen door
and releases him
outdoors

where he abandons warm air,
lights on a boxwood,
sinks into ever shorter days.

For Love of Smallness

When some people dream,
it's of mansions—homes
where rooms stack on top
of each other, a many-tiered
cake frosted with turrets,
ogives, dripping ornamentation.

But I dream the small house
where we lived in those early
years, bedroom barely large
enough to walk around the bed
as we smoothed sheets, fluffed
pillows, and the room where
the baby crib stood, his shelf
of diapers snug against the wall.

I dream a chair with afghan,
one lamp, one cup of tea,
you close by with your singular
devotion, one life scarcely long
enough to hold the enormity of love.

Where I Live

after Maxine Kumin

is hardscrabble: pasture
where stones sprout each winter,
our spring harvest lines fence rows.

    I garden where clay soil's
    stubbornness is mitigated by years
    of mulch—rotted leaves, cow
    and sheep droppings, litter from
    a daughter's pen of Rhode Island reds.

I walk where generations farmed,
rose before dawn to milk and feed,
gather and groom, sweated behind mules,
beast and human equally obstinate.

    Here hawks soar, plaintive calls fill
    the June air, vultures migrate across
    October's vast blueness. Here winter
    suet feeds downy and pileated, tube feeder
    hangs with finch and titmouse.

Here the oak, and here the earth
where children smoothed roads
their toy cars traveled, where stones
lined their make-believe houses,
and minutes fled into years,
the quiet that always waited
enfolding us like a shroud.

III.

In a very real sense, we are the authors of our own lives.

—Mandy Aftel

Ars Specifica

When silence moves
on her little cat feet
through the absences
in your house, offer
her a bed, preferably
where sunlight patches
the room, moves
in its own quiet pattern
down the wall and onto
the braided rug, the one
an elderly aunt created
in her own solitary life,
her nimble fingers stiffening
with the years. Serve
your visitor tea and blue-
berry muffins, the first
rich with the cream
she prefers, and even if
she refuses the muffins,
notice how the berries
stain your hands when
you clear away the dishes,
a blue map you will study
for days to come.

An Arm

after Jane Hirshfield

An arm is not elbow
nor hinge of wrist,
is not muscle tensed
into bulge nor freckled
skin of too many summer suns.

An arm is not power
to pull an engine to life,
strength to lift a stone.
It is not babies it has
gathered safely, old people
who have leaned on it.
It is not swing of axe,
thrash of hoe.
It is not metaphor
for chair part nor
division of the justice system.

The oak's wide arms
shade our afternoons,
house the tanager's nest.
What comes to them arrives
unbidden—sun, rain,
moonlight encasing them
in its earnest embrace.

A Hand, Writing

My handwriting is all over these woods.
—Maggie Smith

As it is over the hills rolling west
toward the Cumberland Plateau,
as it is on the garden where broccoli
and cabbage spread their blue-green
leaves like the smudge my hand makes
as it moves left to right on this crisp sheet
of paper. My writing hand knows not
the carefully curated dish a chef places
before a patron. My hand knows only potatoes,
carrots, onions chopped randomly, browned
in a pot that will clutch peeled tomatoes, a bevy
of sorted vegetables—beans, corn, the surprise
of a yellow crookneck squash, a pinch of salt,
a grind of pepper, a handful of basil or oregano,
maybe thyme. And then the alchemy of heat
and long simmer. My hand writes the bowls
filled to the brim, steam rising, a chunk of bread
where a pat of butter melts into the openness
of yeasty pore, and the figures gathered around
the table, penciled in day by day, each line
a yearning my hand learns as it moves.

Gratitude

It comes to you at twilight,
    the open hand of a grandson
        offering you the day's last strawberry.

It sings with the bluebird
    on the maple limb waiting
        his turn at the bath,
            his kin splashing rainbows
                through the summer air.

It pauses while the first rays
    of sun paint the mountains lilac,
        a neighbor fires his tractor,
            cattle bunched in the pasture,
                their lowing an aubade.

It is the quilt over your legs,
    the cup of tea steaming by your chair,
        a book you'd forgotten you love.

Cats in Sunlight

The cats slumber in afternoon sun,
light ignites orange streaks in their fur,
highlights genes shared by gray tabby
and tortoiseshell sisters.

Daily chores take me in and out
of the room where they lie. My presence
scarcely disturbs them, only a leg twitch

to say *we aren't through here,*
go away until dinner time.

Bless their sleep, O Giver of Longevity,
may their rest add to their lifelines
so that for whatever years my husband
and I have left to totter along this earth,

our cats may remain with us, sleeping
their requisite twenty hours a day in sunlit
patches, curled on our dark bed all night,
snug on the windowsill through rain and snow,

their inert bodies
a reminder—slow down,
slow down, slow down.

Pondering Neruda's "Ode to the Lemon"

What universe is this
that unfolds before us—
the golden barbaric light,
stars that pour congealed
acid, and a planet of fire
where cathedrals and houses,
coasts and markets glimmer
alike in the impossible
taste and feel and smell
of one more small miracle?

Neruda, your watermelons,
artichokes, onions, and tomatoes—
yes, even the blessed wine
and life-giving salt—bow
before the wonder of the lemon,
are arrested in awe that neither
morning light nor heaven's
gift of stars shall equal
the yellow sprite issued
from the lemon tree,
bestowed upon a waiting Earth.

Ode to a Cup of Tea

after Pablo Neruda

My friend
brewed me
a cup of afternoon
tea—amber liquid
in a hand-thrown
mug, earthen brown
vessel holding
the sky,
the constellations
hidden in sunlight,
mug with lip composed
of fossils crushed
into clay, of water
washed from Mount
Vesuvius,
liquid left
from the gods'
last libations,
seep of mint
and sage,
rosemary and thyme,
wild grasses
from the prairie
sweetened by bees,
citizens of the meadow,
purveyors of pollen,
cells of honey stored
against wind and weather,
bears' treasure horde
dissolved
in the near-boil
of the singing
tea kettle.

My friend
sat beside me,
the afternoon's
soft breath,
the labor
of her hands,
she who
stoked the fire
that warmed
the water
that steeped
the tea leaves
that spelled
love
when all
the glad liquid
had slipped down
our happy throats.

Even Today

Language does the best it can.
—Linda Pastan

Even today, sky mute as our aging dog,
I search for words—the *abc*'s of a childhood
when books were a late day treat, when lamplight
softened the room where my coal-mining father—
later, my uranium-enrichment-plant-
working father—and my stay-at-home mother
sat with their open books, pages turning
like the flutter of leaves against the window,
my sisters and I sprawled on the floor, *Childcraft*
volumes open to nursery rhymes or fairytales—
the gingham dog and the calico cat forever
battling while the owl and the pussycat put out
to sea, and Rapunzel lowered her golden
tresses, and language crept upon us, quiet
as the dishes out in the kitchen, the last
vestiges of water drying on their shiny
surfaces where an hour earlier we had
propped them in the rack, each caress of a hand
a benediction on a day's work, the long
evening calling us, and though wordless,
our young selves turned toward language the way
the sun daily turned from ridge to zenith,
and slipped once more into the hollow where
all we loved breathed our same air.

Reach

Strange times reach for strange words.
—Nancy Vala

Though words are no strangers
to me, nor I to them, now that years
have become a long train trailing
my every step, I often reach and reach
again for words, for the names of things
long my companions on this journey—
those innocent nouns hiding in the many
folds of my brain, only a shadow
burrowing deeper as I approach—
dictionary, encyclopedia, novel,
memoir, volume of poetry—
those receptacles where words shine
as they rub against one another,
wells to which I return often,
drink deeply, pour the flood of words
over my body, stretch out in its
sweet flow, my reach and my grasp
at peace with one another for now.

The Lost Poems

How quiet they are there in those drawers,
their pages yellowing, smudged black letters
like tracks of a former life—

    my father home from work, lunchbox clanking
    on the kitchen table, mother peeling potatoes,
    stirring pots of soup that simmer into eternity,

    my children playing cars beneath the oak,
    my husband, grease rag in hand, his
    workshop a cave of metal and imagination.

Who prowls the empty alleys, listens for a step
on the porch? Who will shake out the wrinkles,
smooth memory and awaken dreams, who will

    resurrect iambic pentameter and the snap
    of a sonnet, and who finally will flame the poems
    so sparks drift into our hair, ashes settle on our
    shoulders, a shawl we'll wear into the night?

A Dog-Eared Book

A dog-eared book, like a well-worn pair of loafers,
lies half-hidden beneath the skirt of the chair.

Faded red binding holds the pages safe from stain
and tear, though coffee circles smudge the title.

The dog, lacking opposable thumbs, has eschewed
dog-earing in favor of biting the cover

as a means of sampling what he's heard a book
has to offer. Much larger than a thimble and

infinitely smaller than a whale, this book—
never neon orange, fuchsia, or chartreuse—

reposes in a quiet state far from its home
on the study's book shelves, safe from being

mistaken for a frying pan or an item
to be stored in the freezer, content to clasp

syntax and image, lines wise or lighthearted
that snake between plain frayed covers.

Books

So many line my walls—
good insulation, I tell
my husband when I

carry in another armload,
sufficient ballast to right
any ship set to sail

the windy hilltop
where we live. So many
books to hold in my hands

by a spring window
or tuck on my lap
on the snowiest evening,

sun slowly stealing
away, only words,
words, words to warm

my legs, bring
the world swirling
around my chair,

books stacked higher
than pantry shelves,
more nourishing than

the finest meal—books
a banquet where I feast
day after day.

Afterwards

They don't tell you what lies
beyond Happily Ever After—
how the bones are no longer limber,
how her prince grows a paunch
and what morning breath reeks of.

Not for fairytales the frayed robe
pulled over the raveling nightgown,
its white gone gray with wear. The stories
stop before the first bill comes due,
the checkbook doesn't balance,
and the cupboard is bare as anything
Mother Hubbard and her dog experienced.

And the children—no royalty there
though every two years another head
crowns, and Once Upon a Time begins
anew—the glass slipper or the awakening
kiss waiting out there like a stop light,
the road beyond dark as a villain.

Sky Gazing

Beneath the benign moon
    our pale bodies look up
        into a sky where specks

of light have traveled more
    years than imagination
        can grasp, look up at stars

long dead, look and wonder
    that the universe's
        slow rotation inspired

da Vinci's drawings,
    Galileo's discoveries,
        and we, mere spectators,

lose ourselves in the breadth
    of a cosmos that knows
        no end nor beginning,

a concept that leads us
    to stare, blink, and return
        to the business of sleep.

How You Might Count the Stars

Start with children settled in their beds,
crickets chirping beyond the windows

horses lined on the crest of a hill, wind
in their manes like the fingers of God

a lake reflecting noon sky, surface a mirror
of clouds, trees, and the ancient form of a heron

a leaf-strewn path beneath oak and hickory, squirrels
scolding, crows and jays their own rowdy congregation

a garden fence bordered with sunflowers, marigolds,
the pink of self-sown cleome, a veil of clematis above

morning unfolding from the dark, a bud opening
into petal, pistil, stamen, an egg from embryo to breath

Postcard from Mars

I, a small red body
floating here
where your astronauts

dare not venture,
send greetings to you
there on your hilltop,

telescopes trained
toward me, you
who are manufactured

from dust and minerals
that eons past drifted
free from me

and my sister planets.
You who are figments
of my imagination,

chimera I dream
as I spin
through the universe,

while your eyes
search for light.

Shadow Galaxies

There could be shadow galaxies, shadow stars, and even shadow people.
—Stephen Hawking

The shadow people live on with us,
having left their galaxies, having drifted
from stars that burned through billions
of years, light long dead when it reaches
our eyes—the shadow people, ghosts of all
we dream, gauzy as mist over a lake,
disperse when we approach
or linger at sunset to tease us into one
more moment of longing. Moon and sun
alike welcome them, and only the dense
trees surrounding the house form a moat
they cannot cross and we dare not breach.

Some Small Bone

Some small bone in your foot is longing for heaven.
—Robert Bly

Is longing for what it has not known,
the perfect ease of a body come to rest.
Or perhaps the bone longs for the smoothness
of an angel's wing in flight, feathers fingering
the wind, a lift and rise into the celestial,
soaring where starlight begins and atoms
of hydrogen and oxygen have not yet mated.

Some strand of your hair yearns
after its origin, the root from which
it sprung still secure in your scalp,
a bit of heaven to be so tightly
clasped, so firmly anchored.

Some cell in the ectoplasm of your eyelid
holds a memory of what it was like to be
the first spark of life, first division
that became a multiplication, amoeba-like
body swimming in your mother's sweet
brine—buds of legs, arms, head—
the small bone of your foot where stars
and their billion-year-old light placed it.

The Question of the Unknowable

Sitting beside you tonight as the horizon,
that sweet spot where Earth and sky embrace,
vanishes from sight and stars pop out one
by one—unknown sparks falling into place
to form the familiar constellations, Mars
lingering in the arms of the poplar—I think
back on what brought us here, the years

of struggle, too little money and too many bills,
how morning came with its many tasks, evening
with its blessings, how we had no time to ponder
the unknowable, consumed as we were by children,
jobs, the farm with its urgent, unquenchable demands—
how time rolled us to this moment, time, that

disrespecter of wants and emotions, days vanished
like dry leaves in November wind, like chalk marks
in April rain, like a child's innocence, the two of us
nearing the end of the knowable, filled yet
by the wonder of all that is mysterious.

What Remains

And still we'll have the garden
where gourds climb and wrens
nest in Autumn Clematis.

We'll note the scarlet tanager
on the birdbath, hear
the mockingbird scold the cats,

and all creation breathe
a July afternoon. Beyond
this span we'll yet know

the way poppies spring up
each April, how their petals
crepe-paper the tabletop.

Memory will bear the dark
shadow of the owl
at twilight, how it is

to be small and in an open
field, and yet what sweetness
the honeysuckle,

what joy the bee's probing,
a daffodil's opening,
the silence of the stars.

Praying

Dear Spirit that hides in the kitchen cupboard,
inhabits the soup pot, clatters among the unwashed
dishes, you are the air that dries my sheets
on the clothesline, the mist that moistens
the clematis vine climbing the garden fence,
the breath on the back of my neck,
the squeak on the attic stairs.

I bend my knee to the steady drone
of your demands, to the way bone and body
move through a day, the promise of morning
and resignation of evening. Where you abide
is my cathedral, smudged windows
my stained glass, vacuum cleaner humming
a hymn, my children's faces an open prayer book,

our lives a sacrament we celebrate each holy day—
baptism, marriage, death, the small
rituals of becoming and being,
sunflower into seed for winter birds,
grass into hay, all that grows flowering
and seeding, dying into rising, new vine, new leaf.

Morning

I am silver and exact.
—Sylvia Plath

Flat as the mirror
that hangs on my wall,
this morning lake,
heron on the dock
made double,
my canoe paddle
the only disturbance.

The far bank
spreads a leafy green,
the sun's path a road
my canoe and I travel,
this mirror neither silver
nor exact, but a shifting
surface where all
that's reflected
comes back softer,
more gentle
than the real world
could ever be.

Good

You do not have to be good.
—Mary Oliver

You do not have to walk on your knees
nor do you have to relive the shortcomings
of your youth, your young adulthood,
the way ageing deprives your body of its
resilience, your mind often muddled.
Look how sunrise ignites the tips
of the maples, their true colors emerging
day by day as the chlorophyll of their
summer vigor withdraws. Step into
an October morning alive with birds
in their migration. See how the finch
settles into his somber winter coat,
how he does not mourn the bright gold
of his summer plumage, how even
the sky shines with a new dawn,
and this evening stars will once more
pierce the darkness, light that is neither
good nor bad, is merely a beacon of what
is and has been through human memory,
how Earth in her changing will go on
circling the sun, spinning through space.

Myth of the Fish

We must risk delight.
—Jack Gilbert

That summer, sun sparked fire
on the lake's surface—it was
that hot. A fish came to live
beneath the boat dock, to slip out
and swim beside me as I stroked
back and forth, shallow water
to deep, the fish a slender silvery
shadow of my buoyant body.

If this were a tall tale, the fish
would have lifted me, carried me
across the lake to a school of her kin,
where my shoulder blades would become
gills, learn to draw oxygen from water,
my legs fused into a willowy oneness
whipping me through the waves.

But this is a story of how it was
to know only mystery, how every
time I entered the water, the fish was
there, how summer passed in quiet
pleasure, how joy sometimes just is.

Acknowledgments

Deepest gratitude to the editors of the following journals where poems in this collection, some in slightly different form, earlier appeared:

Anthology of Appalachian Writers: "Bless It All," "Chicken Psalm," "Earth, Always Earth," "The Family That Dances Together," "Good," "McCrory's Five and Ten," "My Sister Points Out the Obvious," "Portrait of a Young Girl Peeling Potatoes," "Scattered," "Tell Me About Driving," "Those Others," "What Never Happened"

Artemis Journal: "Nameless as the Minnows," "Tell Me How You Were Wild and Green in the Ways of the World"

The Aurorean: "Tractor"

Black Moon Magazine: "Help," "Reach," "Watching"

Bluestone Review: "A Dog-Eared Book," "To Sleeplessness"

Bloodroot: "Books," "Learning to Shift Gears," "The Lost Poems"

Connecticut River Review: "Where I Live"

Cumberland Review River: "Praying"

Floyd County Moonshine: "Afterwards"

Heartwood Literary Magazine: "Car Trip"

In God's Hand: "What Remains"

I Thought I Heard a Cardinal Sing: Ohio's Appalachian Voices, edited by Kari Gunter-Seymour: "The Worker's Story" (Sheila-Na-Gig Editions, 2022)

Jelly Bucket: "Shadow Galaxies"

Mildred Haun Review: "Dish Towel," "Clothes Drying in the Sun" (originally "Sweet Joy of Clothes Drying on the Line"), "Hungry for Love"

Pigeon Parade Quarterly: "Moving to Tennessee, 1944"

Pine Mountain Sand & Gravel: "First Death," "Looking Back," "Morning," "Myth of the Fish," "Witness"

Poem: "Feeding"

Potomac Review: "Even Today," "The Question of Where" (nominated for a Pushcart Prize)

Shift: "Cats in Sunlight," "Change Coming"

Smallish Blog (Evelyn Rennich): "For Love of Smallness"

Still: The Journal: "Ars Specifica," "Sky Gazing," "Some Small Bone"

Time of Singing: "Gratitude"; Elegies Contest, first place: "There Was: An Elegy for My Father"; Editor's Choice Elegies Contest: "Elegy for My Mother"

Tiny Seed Literary Journal: "The December Bee," "Postcard from Mars," "Trust as Synonym for Gardener"

Voices on the Wind: "An Arm," "Eight Ways of Looking at Loss," "A Hand, Writing," "Pondering Neruda's 'Ode to the Lemon'"

Whale Road Review: "On Not Remembering"

Women Speak, edited by Kari Gunter-Seymour: "The Question of the Unknowable," "Rocks," "Moving to the Country" (Sheila-Na-Gig Editions, 2022, 2024)

"How You Might Count the Stars" was awarded first place in the Poetry Society of Tennessee annual contest, 2021, and published in *Tennessee Voices*.

"Ode to a Cup of Tea" was awarded first place in the Knoxville Writers Guild annual poetry contest, 2022, and published at knoxvillewritersguild.org.

About the Author

Connie Jordan Green is the author of novels for young people, *The War at Home* and *Emmy*; poetry chapbooks, *Slow Children Playing* and *Regret Comes to Tea*; and collections, *Household Inventory* (2015 Brick Road Poetry Prize) and *Darwin's Breath*; and a personal newspaper column that ran for more than 42 years. Her poetry and prose have appeared in numerous journals and anthologies. She is the recipient of awards for her writing, including induction into the East Tennessee Writers Hall of Fame, a Tribute to the Arts Award from the Oak Ridge Arts Council, and inclusion in *Listen Here: Women Writing in Appalachia* (University Press of Kentucky, 2003). She taught creative writing for the University of Tennessee and continues to teach at various workshops.

www.ingramcontent.com/pod-product-compliance
Lightning Source LLC
Chambersburg PA
CBHW032056090426
42744CB00005B/237